W9-ACY-045

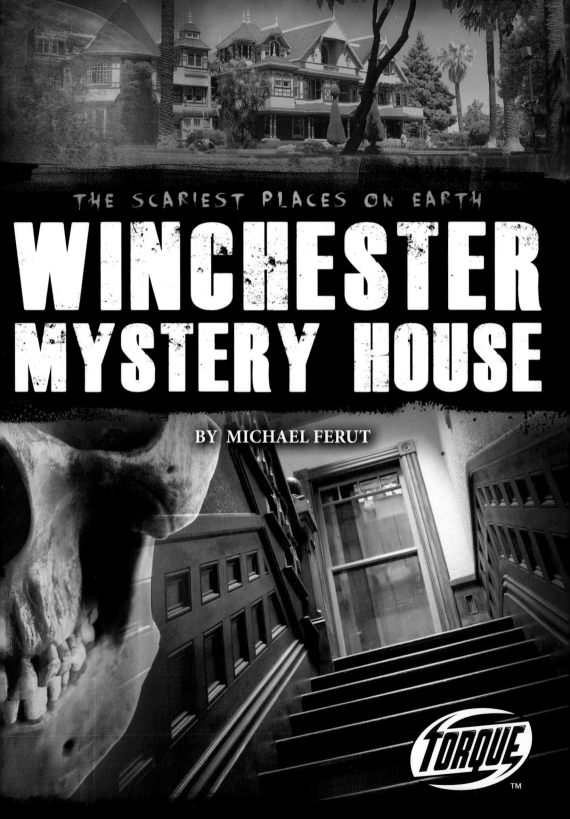

THE SCARIEST PLACES ON EARTH

WINCHESTER MYSTERY HOUSE

BY MICHAEL FERUT

TORQUE™

BELLWETHER MEDIA · MINNEAPOLIS, MN

Are you ready to take it to the extreme?
Torque books thrust you into the action-packed world
of sports, vehicles, mystery, and adventure. These
books may include dirt, smoke, fire, and chilling tales.
WARNING : read at your own risk.

Library of Congress Cataloging-in-Publication Data

Ferut, Michael, author.
  Winchester Mystery House / by Michael Ferut.
      pages cm. -- (Torque. The Scariest Places on Earth)
  Summary: "Engaging images accompany information about the Winchester Mystery House.
The combination of high-interest subject matter and light text is intended for students in grades
3 through 7"-- Provided by publisher.
  Audience: Ages 7-12.
  Audience: Grades 3 to 7.
  Includes bibliographical references and index.
  ISBN 978-1-60014-998-6 (hardcover : alk. paper)
  1. Winchester, Sarah Pardee, 1837-1922--Juvenile literature. 2. Winchester Mystery House (San Jose,
Calif.)--Juvenile literature. 3. Ghosts--California--San Jose--Juvenile literature. 4. Haunted houses--
California--San Jose--Juvenile literature. 5. San Jose (Calif.)--Legends--Juvenile literature. I. Title. II.
Series: Torque (Minneapolis, Minn.) III. Series: Scariest places on earth.
  BF1472.U6F475 2014
  133.1'29794'74--dc23
                                                2013050263

This edition first published in 2015 by Bellwether Media, Inc.

Printed in the United States of America, North Mankato, MN.

TABLE OF CONTENTS

CHAPTER 1

A MAZE IN A MANSION

It seems like you have been lost for hours. Nothing in this house makes sense. Stairs lead to ceilings. Doors open to blank walls.

Your footsteps echo throughout the empty mansion. Floorboards creak beneath your feet. Nobody else is around, but you feel like you are being followed.

You walk faster. Then you see a shadow creeping around a corner. You try to run, but the halls twist and turn too much.

You see a door ahead and rush to open it. Fresh air! But there is a huge drop down to the ground. The shadow inches closer. Do you jump?

CHAPTER 2

FROM HUNTING TO HAUNTING

The Winchester Mystery House was built by Sarah Winchester. She was the wife of the Connecticut businessman William Winchester. He made a lot of money selling guns to hunters and settlers. Then tragedies struck the Winchesters.

Sarah Winchester

San José

California

N
W—E
S

Sarah and William had a young daughter named Annie. She died unexpectedly. Then William died from **tuberculosis**. Sarah was very sad. In 1886, she moved to San José, California for a new start.

Many believe a **psychic** told Sarah to build a mansion. The psychic said the spirits of those killed by Winchester rifles haunted Sarah's family. To satisfy the spirits, she was told to build them a house. The psychic said she would die if she stopped building.

WINCHESTER'S NEW GUN

The Winchester rifle shot more bullets in less time than other guns. It was very deadly. Many Native Americans and western settlers were killed with this rifle.

WINCHESTER
MODEL 55 .30 CAL.

11

LUCKY NUMBER THIRTEEN

Some think thirteen is unlucky or scary. Sarah liked it, though. She often built things in sets of thirteen. These included stairs, bathrooms, and windowpanes.

Sarah bought an old farmhouse with a lot of land. For thirty-eight years, she added unusual rooms and passages on to the house. Construction went on day and night. Today, the house has about 160 different rooms.

Some think Sarah designed the house to confuse bad spirits. They would get lost in the maze of halls, sudden drops, and dead ends. Meanwhile, Sarah and friendly spirits would be kept safe.

DOOR TO NOWHERE

CHAPTER 3

VISITORS FROM BEYOND?

Sarah had few visitors when she was alive. But after she died, people noticed many strange things happening in the mansion. They heard breathing or footsteps in empty rooms. Some reported hearing organ music. Many saw things they could not explain.

15

One worker at the house seemed to be the target of ghostly pranks. Doors that he had just locked would unlock themselves. Lights that he had turned off would turn back on. One time, he showed up at work to find his desk covered in water. The rest of the room was dry.

LOYAL WORKER

A caretaker once saw a man pushing a wheelbarrow in the basement. But no other workers were down there that day. Then, more people saw the same man in the basement. No one knew who he was. Finally, someone saw him in an old photo. He was one of the builders Sarah hired more than 100 years before!

17

Sarah Winchester's bedroom

Today, the house is open to **tourists**. Many say that two particular rooms are the most **eerie**. People often feel Sarah's presence in the bedroom where she died. The **séance** room is also said to be full of spirits.

In these rooms, visitors often feel like they are being watched. Some people feel a hand on their shoulder when no one is there. Others feel very cold, even in the summer.

THE FURNITURE IN THIS ROOM
WAS DONATED BY:
MR. & MRS. W. C. THOMPSON

THE HEIRLOOM CENTENNIAL QUILT
WAS DESIGNED & DONATED BY
THE SANTA CLARA VALLEY QUILT
ASSOCIATION

WE THANK THEM FOR THEIR GENEROSITY

séance room

Much about Sarah Winchester and her mansion is unknown. But there are many chilling stories about the house. Is it haunted or just odd? Maybe the best way to find out is to visit the mansion yourself. Make sure to leave before it closes, though. You might not want to spend the night.

GLOSSARY

eerie—strange and scary

psychic—someone who is said to tell the future or speak with the dead

séance—an attempt to talk with spirits of dead people

settlers—people who go to live in a new place where no or few others live

tourists—people who travel to visit another place

tragedies—disastrous events that cause great sadness

tuberculosis—an often deadly disease that affects the lungs

AT THE LIBRARY

Claybourne, Anna. *100 Scariest Things on the Planet*. New York, N.Y.: Scholastic, Inc., 2011.

Stone, Adam. *Haunted Houses*. Minneapolis, Minn.: Bellwether Media, 2011.

Von Finn, Denny. *Stanley Hotel*. Minneapolis, Minn.: Bellwether Media, 2014.

ON THE WEB

Learning more about the Winchester Mystery House is as easy as 1, 2, 3.

1. Go to www.factsurfer.com.

2. Enter "Winchester Mystery House" into the search box.

3. Click the "Surf" button and you will see a list of related web sites.

With factsurfer.com, finding more information is just a click away.

INDEX